THOMAS WILFRED

PROJECTED   SCENERY

A TECHNICAL MANUAL

DRAMA BOOK SPECIALISTS/PUBLISHERS

New York

Printed in U.S.A. by
NOBLE OFFSET PRINTERS, INC.
New York, N.Y. 10003

TABLE OF CONTENTS

INTRODUCTION

Projected Scenery is a basic new method of Stage Decoration.

Instead of painted and lighted backdrops that must be changed for each new setting, a permanent white screen or cyclorama is substituted and the different settings are projected onto this screen by means of powerful scenic projectors of various types.

Projected Scenery is not a universal substitute for painted and built scenery; in certain cases it is not even practical. Rather is it a new tool in the hand of the designer. When used with discrimination, it can yield results hitherto unobtainable, while at the same time simplifying the staging of a play and cutting the production cost considerably.

The use of projected scenery will be particularly advantageous to Repertory Theatres, Educational Theatres, and theatres lacking facilities for painting, building and storing conventional scenery.

In Arena Theatres projected scenery may now be used on a large scale to surround actor and audience alike with atmospheric settings.

Projected Scenery can give a greater illusion of size and depth in a setting. It permits not only rapid changes but also gradual transition from one setting to the next; or from daylight, through sunset, to night, or the reverse, with the same setting. It permits mobility, from drifting clouds to purely fantastic effects. Finally, it permits the lighting artist at the control board to blend setting and actor-lighting together, as a painter balances light, shade, and accent on his canvas. The result may be termed VISUAL ACCOMPANIMENT TO SPEECH AND ACTION.

With the advent of projected scenery there is something new to learn for Director, Designer, and Technician alike, but once the new medium has been mastered it will open up a vast new field of possibilities.

Consult GLOSSARY for definitions of optical and other unusual terms in text. An elementary knowledge of optics is useful to a technician but not necessary to a designer.

Books and Magazine Articles dealing with the subject are listed in BIBLIOGRAPHY.

Under MANUFACTURERS are listed many of the firms supplying Scenic Projectors, as well as Materials and Supplies used for settings.

PROJECTION METHODS

REAR PROJECTION on TRANSLUCENT SCREEN located between projector and acting area.

FRONT PROJECTION on OPAQUE SCREEN located as far upstage as possible.

Both systems have advantages and drawbacks, and the choice of either must depend on factors such as depth of stage, size of screen or cyclorama, height of flyspace, repertory, and last but not least, available funds.

A very deep stage with full flyspace and equipped with several cycloramas may be equipped with both REAR and FRONT systems. The Paris Opera for example, with its enormous stage, has a large booth built into the rear stage wall for REAR projection, a downstage lightbridge with 3 lens projectors for FRONT projection, and a second booth built into a fifth tier auditorium box for FRONT projection on large downstage gauze drops.

As a general rule, REAR projection is practical only on stages 46 feet in depth or deeper and with full flyspace to permit the delicate translucent screen to be hoisted up out of harm's reach when not in use. In the United States such stage dimensions are rarely found. FRONT projection will therefore be advisable, if not necessary, in the majority of cases.

On small stages lacking flyspace, or scene dock, or both, projected scenery will permit a repertory of productions which before were out of the question.

Because of the greater depth-illusion characteristic of good projected settings, they can make any stage appear more spacious.

There is much new to be learned by designer and technician, and perfect results should not be expected at the outset; the many new possibilities will be discovered and utilized gradually. The convenience of being able to store an entire season's scenery in a filing cabinet, ready for instant use, will be appreciated, as will the considerable drop in production cost.

The Comparison Plans on the following page will give a better picture of the factors involved in REAR and FRONT projection.

IMPORTANT. Scenic projectors must not be classified as odd items to be acquired from time to time when funds permit, as you would buy an extra spot or an extra dimmer. A carefully planned installation is absolutely essential for professional results. Its cost should be written off as a long-term expenditure which, in time, will more than pay for itself; as you would naturally classify the installation of a new switchboard or fly-rigging.

The first complete installation of scenic projection equipment in the United States, in the University Playhouse (University of Washington) in Seattle, Washington, has been a decided success from all points of view, artistically, technically, and financially.

Here, as in every other field of endeavor, half-hearted attempts, with inadequate equipment and knowledge, are inadvisable.

COMPARISON PLANS OF REAR AND FRONT PROJECTION METHODS WITH IDENTICAL BASIC DIMENSIONS OF PROJECTOR, SCREEN, ACTING AREA, AND PROSCENIUM IN BOTH PLANS

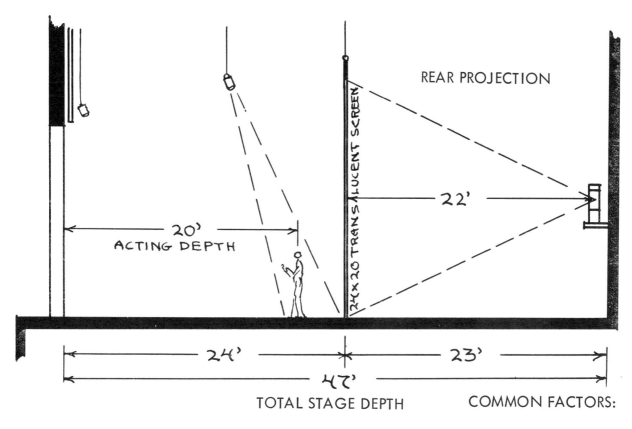

REAR PROJECTION

24 x 20 TRANSLUCENT SCREEN

22'

20'
ACTING DEPTH

24'

23'

47'

TOTAL STAGE DEPTH

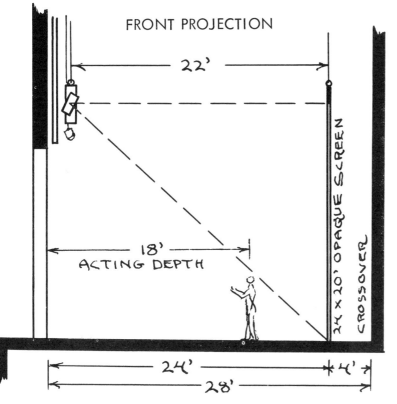

FRONT PROJECTION

22'

24 x 20' OPAQUE SCREEN

CROSSOVER

18'
ACTING DEPTH

24'

4'

28'

COMMON FACTORS:

PROJECTOR: 5000 W. MULTIPLATE LATERAL TYPE. PLATES: 5 x 6 "
OBJECTIVE: 126 mm MAGNALUX f:2
PROJECTION DISTANCE: 22'
PROSCENIUM TO SCREEN: 24'
PROSCENIUM HEIGHT: 16'

In REAR PROJECTION, the practical acting depth is 20' if actor is to be lit from proper angle. Closer to screen the actor lighting will hit the screen as well and pale the projected image. Only in a scene acted in silhouette can the actor work right up to the screen.

In FRONT PROJECTION, the practical acting depth is 18'. Closer to the screen the actor would enter the projection beam and cast a shadow.

The extra 19' in stage depth required for REAR PROJECTION thus adds only two feet to the useful acting area depth.

REAR PROJECTION

Rear Projection is thus practical only on fairly deep stages, or on shallower stages where a central scene dock, prop room, or dressing room behind the stage permits location of a projector far to the rear. In any case, the projection equipment must be of the wide-angle type.

With a Lens Projector the widest possible angle at present is 58 degrees horizontally. This means that in order to obtain a projected image 24 feet wide, the projector front must be located 22 feet from the translucent screen.

With a direct Beam Projector a 90-degree angle of spread is possible, and a 24 feet wide image could therefore be achieved from a distance of only 12 feet, but the wider the angle of spread, the greater the loss of image intensity from the center outward toward edges. Between 58 and 70 degrees may be considered practical.

An opaque screen arrests the projected light on its surface and, if properly made, yields practically 100% of the intensity it receives.

A translucent screen transmits the light and, in doing so, absorbs up to one-half of the initial intensity from the projector. The projector must therefore be powerful enough to make up for the transmission loss. Translucent screens are made in varying densities. The lesser the density the more brilliant the image will appear to the central section of the seating area but the more dim to spectators on the extreme sides. A screen density transmitting 40 - 50% of the projected light is recommended for stage purposes. Translucent screens transmitting up to 75% are used in Television, but here the camera is the sole spectator and may be located along the optical axis where the image is of maximum intensity.

The best translucent screens are now made of plastics. They are sold by two principal companies, THE TRANS-LUX CORPORATION in New York City, and THE BODDE SCREEN CO. in Los Angeles. Trans-lux screens can be had in sizes up to 48 x 98 feet without seams. Price about $ 2.50 per square foot. The average backdrop size, 25 x 30 feet, will thus cost $ 1.850.

Another type of translucent screen can be made right on the stage from "Hansen Cloth" which comes 30 feet wide and in any length. This fabric must be dipped in a solution of powdered Vinylite plastic in a liquid solvent. A trough must be made, a little longer than the screen width, the solution poured in, the screen lowered into it on a set of lines and then hoisted up to dry. When dry, the screen may be rolled on a round pole at least 4" in diameter. It can not be folded.

Translucent screens are expensive and vulnerable. A stain or tear can not be invisibly repaired. A toppling flat, a too enthusiastic extra with a spear, and you buy a new screen. The Mica or Glass powder sometimes dusted on to increase diffusion gives a tinsel-like, "Christmas Card" quality to the projected setting.

FRONT PROJECTION

Front Projection utilizes the space over the acting area, thus making "double depth" unnecesary. On a stage of average proportions the ideal location for the projection equipment is directly over first border, close to the fire curtain. From this location the lower limit of the projection beam will travel to the bottom of the screen or cyclorama at such an angle that an actor can move to within his own height of the screen without entering the beam. (See Comparison Plans.)

If no actor moves closer to the screen than approximately five feet, action over the rest of the stage can be adequately lighted without ever interfering with the projected setting.

BRIDGE INSTALLATION is preferable for a number of reasons enumerated below; the principal of these being easier access to the projectors, and storage space for settings and supplies near projectors.

SUSPENSION INSTALLATION is now possible with the latest projector types. A Multiplate lens projector is available with lateral optical system, and capable of projecting ten different settings by remote control. Clamped onto a two-inch pipe batten, this projector requires only 12 inches of depth, or about as much as the first border itself over which it is hung. Direct Beam projectors may be clamped onto the same batten on either side of the Multiplate unit. This batten is located directly over first border but hung on an independent set of lines. First border may thus be raised or lowered without moving the projectors. By this method no useful space is lost over the stage. All other line sets may be used for scenery.

PROJECTION SURFACE. A permanent plaster cyclorama is preferable. If desired, it may be curved at extreme sides but the center section should be left plane to avoid cross-diffusion from one part of the surface to the rest. This tends to lessen contrast in the projected image and causes distortion.

A sand-finished surface is best. If plaster has dried unevenly or has shiny patches, a coat of white Calsomine will produce a perfect surface yielding 100% diffusion, and reflecting almost 100% of the initial light.

An ordinary backdrop will serve where a plaster screen is impractical. Its surface should be flat white and free from wrinkles. Do not use Mica or glass powder coating as this will produce the same tinsel-like quality observable on similarly treated translucent screens.

Opaque screens are comparatively inexpensive. They are easily repaired or touched up. With care they will last almost indefinitely.

A plaster screen or cyclorama also provides an excellent sound shield where dressing rooms are located behind stage.

PERSONAL NOTES

THE PROJECTION EQUIPMENT

LENS PROJECTORS, in their simplest form, represent only improvements and refinements of the age-old lantern slide projector with a lightsource, a condenser system, a focal plane for the image plate, and an objective. They are used where a sharply defined screen image is desired and should generally be of the wide-angle type. Three basic models are used.

UNIPLATE PROJECTOR. The simplest type. Holds one plate (slide) only. Changes must be made manually.

MULTIPLATE PROJECTOR holds up to ten plates on a multiple rotating plate-holder. A change from one plate to the next is effected by pushbutton from the control board, or from any other remote point.

EFFECT ATTACHMENT, or "Dutchman," converts a standard 1000-2000 watt spot into a lens projector. The spot lens serves as rear condenser element, and the attachment consists of a front condenser element, a focal plane for either plates or rotating disc effects (clouds, fog, rain, fire, etc.) and an uncorrected objective. For the projection of designs with sharp detail, such as architectural subjects, an Anastigmatic objective is substituted.

LENSLESS PROJECTORS. The latest development in this field is the Direct Beam Projector in which design elements can be interposed in several planes, taking advantage of the fact that the greatest diffusion is obtained nearest the lamp, the greatest sharpness farthest from the lamp. By this method a much better depth-illusion can be obtained, from a soft and distant sky to a sharp foreground object. Absolute sharpness, comparable to that of a lens projector, is not at present obtainable. New lamps may change this. For a number of years the well-known Linnebach Lantern, with its single-plane glass plate, was the only lensless model available. It had its great limitations. The frequently heard "we tried projected scenery and it didn't work" could all too often be traced to this rigid apparatus.

SPECIAL PROJECTORS. For effects not obtainable with above projector types, especially mobile and non-objective backgrounds, several Clavilux models have been designed by the author for theatre use, such as:

THE REFLECTION PROJECTOR, consisting of a moving light source, a rotating color record, and a series of mirrors which may be moved through varying orbits. This projector is suitable only for fantastic mobile effects.

THE FOCAL-STAGE PROJECTOR is a lens projector, but with an optical system permitting the use of three-dimensional settings in motion. This unit is also best suited for fantastic effects. It is capable of creating mobile sequences of changing form and color with a peculiar quality of depth and solidity.

Several projectors may be used for one setting. A basic sky and mountain background, for example, may be projected from a Direct Beam unit which leaves the lower part of the screen dark. Upon this dark area various foregrounds may be added from a lens projector to represent different locations in the mountain country. This method was used with excellent results in PEER GYNT by Professor John Ashby Conway at the University of Washington.

PERSONAL NOTES

THE LENS PROJECTOR

A scenic lens projector is merely a specially constructed lantern slide projector. The special construction is necessary for several reasons. A scenic projector must generally have a wider projection angle for covering a larger screen area from a short projection distance. It must also have a more efficient cooling system for preventing plate damage. A lantern slide is rarely projected for more than a minute at a time, but a projected setting may have to be used throughout the entire play, perhaps during four acts of 20 minutes each. Finally, a scenic projector must generally have a very strong light source if the projected setting is to hold its own against unavoidable spills and reflections of light from the acting area.

All lens projectors contain two separate but completely interdependent optical systems, Condenser system and Objective system. (See lower plan diagram of Multiplate projector on page 9.)

CONDENSER. The condenser system here consists of three elements (single plano-convex lenses) 8, 9, 10. Its purpose is to pick up the light from lamp 6 and to shape it into a beam of sufficient diameter to illuminate the entire surface of the plate in the focal plane 11, upon which the setting to be projected has been painted or photographed, and then to converge all the rays in this beam to a Nodal Point (where the rays cross, thus reversing the image).

OBJECTIVE. The objective consists of several elements mounted in a metal barrel which again slides in a metal sleeve to permit focusing. The purpose of the objective is to pick up the illuminated image on the plate and to transmit it, greatly enlarged, to the screen.

FOCAL LENGTH. Each objective has a definite Focal Length, the distance from the Nodal Point in the objective to the plate surface in the Focal Plane. The shorter the focal length of an objective, the wider its projection angle and the larger the image it is capable of projecting from a given distance.

It will now be obvious that condenser and objective systems must work together in order to transmit a maximum amount of light from lamp to screen. The condenser system must therefore be so designed that its nodal point coincides with the nodal point of the objective system. In other words, the objective transmits the beam of light from condenser to screen and, in doing so, also transmits a sharp image of the design on the plate.

ANASTIGMATIC OBJECTIVE. In order to transmit a sharp and undistorted image, the objective must be Anastigmatic (corrected for both line and color distortion) hence the several elements in the barrel, usually three, the two outside ones ground from Crown Glass, the middle one from Flint Glass. Without delving too deeply into optics, it can be stated here that each kind of glass has optical imperfections, that the imperfections of Crown and Flint glass go, as it were, in opposite directions, and that by using lenses of both kinds in an objective the imperfections of one kind will neutralize those of the other when properly balanced.

The anastigmatic objective is a "must" in a good lens projector.

THE MULTIPLATE PROJECTOR

LATERAL SUSPENSION MODEL

5000 Watt lamp. Capacity, ten 5 x 6" plates on motor-driven rotor. Cooling by two 100 CFM blowers and heat-absorbing filter. Objective. f:2, 126 mm MAGNALUX. Angle of coverage 70 degrees. Color Modifier. (See plans on opposite page.)

Measuring only twelve inches in depth when clamped onto a standard 2" pipe batten directly over first light border, the projector occupies an otherwise unusable space over the stage, leaving all adjacent line sets free, and instantly available for the projection of up to ten different settings.

On the plans the projector is shown clamped onto a 2" pipe batten 1 by means of two heavy-duty pipe clamps 2. The lamphouse 3 has an upper inspection door 4 in lamp chamber and a lower door in blower chamber 5. In the lower diagrammatic view from above, 6 is the 5000 watt lamp and its spherical aluminum mirror. The intermediate condenser chamber 7 contains rear condenser element 8 with heat absorbing filter and Color Modifier, middle element 9 (10" diameter) and front element 10. 11 is one of the ten plates mounted on rotor 12 which revolves around a smaller central chamber containing the Magnalux objective 13 and the first-surface mirror 14. In upper front elevation at left 15 is the plate-cooling blower. The projection chamber 16 is completely sealed against dust when projector is not in use, by means of the double-vaned electric shutter 17 which opens automatically when main breaker is turned on and closes again when current is turned off. The entire assembly is mounted in aluminum chassis 19 which permits the projection chamber 16 to be tilted up to 22 degrees either way while lamphouse and chassis remain vertical. Inspection door 18 in base of projection chamber permits instant removal and exchange of plates on rotor 12. Pilot lamps illuminate the interior for inspection and plate changes. Entire front **panel** of chamber 16 is removable for **adjustments.**

The cooling system is so efficient that an Ektachrome color film will show no appreciable fading after prolonged continuous projection, the cover glasses remaining cool to the touch at all times.

The Color Modifier permits slow, almost imperceptible transitions from day, through sunset, to night, or vice-versa, with any suitable plate, an effect mere dimming can not accomplish. Two frames with colors fused in glass move in opposite directions, driven by a small reversible motor and gear assembly. Control of Modifier and plate changer is effected through low-tension wires from any remote point.

This projector is equally well suited for mounting on a permanent light bridge. If used for Rear Projection, it may be permanently mounted on the upstage wall opposite exact **center** of the translucent screen, thus eliminating distortion. In this location the beam of light will be reflected from the mirror as if it actually issued from the surface of the wall, with not a foot lost.

Weight of complete projector: 145 lbs.

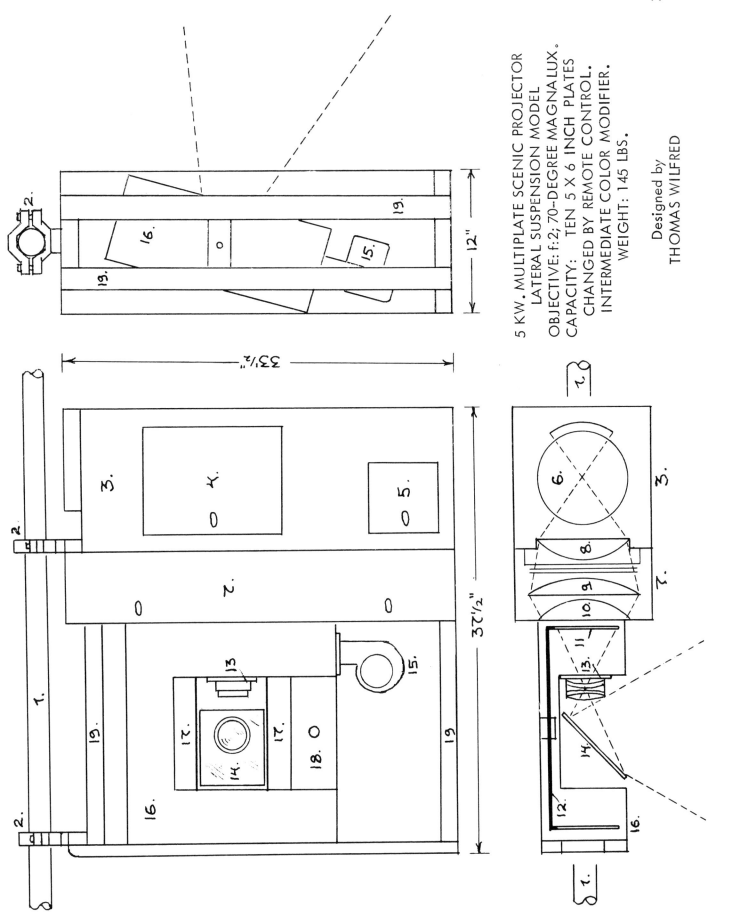

5 KW. MULTIPLATE SCENIC PROJECTOR
LATERAL SUSPENSION MODEL
OBJECTIVE: f:2; 70-DEGREE MAGNALUX.
CAPACITY: TEN 5 x 6 INCH PLATES
CHANGED BY REMOTE CONTROL.
INTERMEDIATE COLOR MODIFIER.
WEIGHT: 145 LBS.

Designed by
THOMAS WILFRED

PERSONAL NOTES

APERTURE. The Aperture, or diameter, of the objective is important. The larger the aperture, the more light is transmitted with the image to the screen. Aperture is measured in its relation to the focal length. The largest practical aperture at present is one-half of the focal length, and is variously designated 1:2, or f:2. The smallest advisable aperture in a projection objective is one-sixth of the focal length, or f:6.

ANGLE OF COVERAGE. This refers to the relation between the focal length of an objective and the diameter of the circular field it is capable of transmitting. It is frequently assumed that if a lantern slide objective has the proper focal length and aperture, it will serve equally well in a projector designed for much larger plates, but in most cases its angle of coverage will not be wide enough to include the corners of the larger plate. It must therefore always be ascertained that the objective is capable of transmitting a circular field as large in diameter as the diagonal of the effective plate area is long. Example: Focal length is 5" and plate size 5 x 6". The effective picture area of a 5 x 6" plate (minus 1/4" along all four sides for binding tape and framing) is a 4-1/2 x 5-1/2" rectangle with its diagonal 7-1/16" long. Lines drawn from the ends of the diagonal to the nodal point will meet at an angle of 70 degrees and represent the Angle of Coverage required in the objective if it is to render a sharp screen image of the entire plate area.

To sum up. In order to transmit a sharp, undistorted, and bright image of proper size, the objective must possess the following properties.

CORRECT FOCAL LENGTH. Method for determining this described on page 12.

SUFFICIENT APERTURE. Preferably f:2, not less than f:6, average f:4.

SUFFICIENT ANGLE OF COVERAGE. Capable of transmitting entire plate area.

ANASTIGMATIC DESIGN. Corrected for line and color distortion.

PROJECTOR CONSTRUCTION

If a lens projector is to be practical for scenic work it must have a strong and well-designed housing to protect all optical and mechanical parts, keep out dust and grime, and prevent light from escaping in unwanted directions. Most scenic projectors are designed for 2000 to 5000 watt lamps which generate considerable heat. Adequate cooling must be provided in the lamphouse, in the beam of light, and around the plate. A 5000 watt lamphouse should have a 100 CFM (cubic feet per minute) blower built into its base, with the blast directed upward around lamp and socket. A large and light-proof exhaust opening should be provided in the top of the lamphouse. A second 50 CFM blower should be located near the plate, with the blast directed over its surface. Much of the heat in the beam of light itself can now be eliminated by the insertion of a Heat-absorbing Filter made from special glass and generally located between first and second condenser elements. To lessen heat-transmission, the lamphouse should have as little surface contact with the rest of the projector as possible. With the above precautions taken, a projector should produce an image of sufficient brilliancy without damage to even a sensitive Ektachrome color plate during prolonged projection. Some of the intensity is sacrificed in the process of heat elimination but this is unavoidable.

PERSONAL NOTES

MAINTENANCE. Dust and grime are the greatest enemies of a lens projector. Even with the most efficient housing, all optical surfaces should be cleaned frequently by an expert hand. Dirty lamps, filters, and plates will not only blur the projected setting but also generate extra and unnecessary heat wherever the beam of light passes. During productions not using projection all units should be covered with dustproof hoods.

SELECTING THE PROPER PROJECTOR

For all Rear Projection a 5000 watt projector with 5 x 6" plates is recommended beaause of the considerable loss of intensity through even the best translucent screen.

For Front Projection distances up to 18 feet, and screens no larger than 20 x 16 feet, a 2000 watt projector will generally serve. For longer distances and larger screens a 5000 watt projector is recommended.

Where it is practical to station an operator by the projector, a Uniplate Projector (single plate, manual change) will serve. In all other cases a Multiplate Projector (up to ten plates, automatic change) should be selected. If the projector is to be suspended from a batten, it should further be a lateral type with the optical system parallel to the batten and a 45-degree mirror directing the beam toward the screen.

A wide-angle objective will be needed in most cases. The widest angle of coverage at this writing is 70 degrees (Magnalux f:2). This means that the objective is capable of projecting a circular image 31 feet in diameter from a distance of 22 feet, or any rectangular image within the limits of the circle, for example 24' 3" wide and 20' 3" high which means a spread of 58 degrees horizontally and 49 degrees vertically. Even this may not be wide enough if the screen is large and the distance limited. Two projectors may then be used, each covering one-half of the screen. In this case the two units should be adjusted to have their images overlap as much as possible in the center area in order that the two halves of the setting may be blended together gradually and imperceptibly.

It is almost impossible to join two sharply outlined halves without leaving an annoying vertical division line.

If it is not possible to use two lens projectors the only solution is to substitute a Direct Beam projector which, if properly designed, can cover a 90-degree angle both vertically and horizontally.

A lens projector should be designed for a large plate. The 5 x 6" size is recommended for the following reasons.
1. Its proportions coincide with those of the standard backdrop.
2. The larger optical system it requires transmits more light from lamp.
3. Its larger effective area facilitates hand-painting of settings.
4. The standard 5 x 7" Ektachrome color film and the standard 5 x 7" photographic cover glass may be used with trimming of length only.
5. Heat is distributed over a larger area and more efficiently dissipated.
6. The larger image area gives a sharper rendition of detail.

PERSONAL NOTES

METHOD FOR DETERMINING THE PROJECTOR TYPE NEEDED WITH SCREEN SIZE AND PROJECTION DISTANCE DETERMINED OR SCREEN SIZES AND PROJECTION DISTANCES POSSIBLE WITH A PROJECTOR ALREADY AT HAND

EXAMPLE: Screen is 24' wide and Projection Distance 22' (left). The extended Projection Angle from Nodal Point of Objective into Projector (right) indicates that if your Plate Size is 3-1/4" × 4" (Standard Lantern Slide), your useful Horizontal Plate Area (minus Binding Tape around edges) is 3-1/2", and the Objective should therefore have a Focal Length of 3-1/4". If you want a larger Projector with 5×6" Plates, you will need an Objective with a Focal Length of 5". If you want a 30' wide Screen, you must increase the Projection Distance to 27'6". The only constant factor is the Horizontal Projection angle which in this example is 57 degrees.

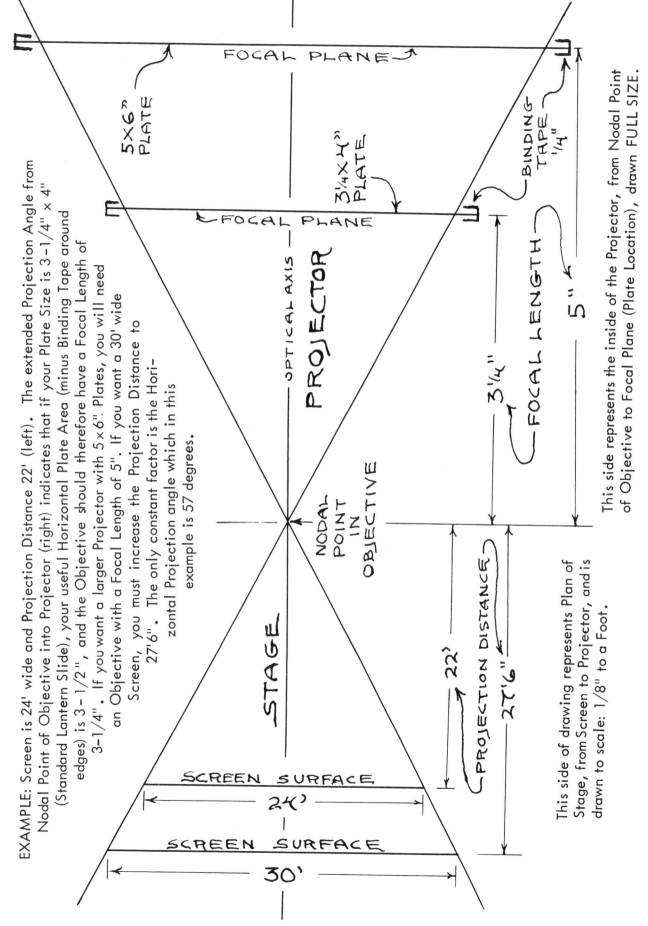

This side of drawing represents Plan of Stage, from Screen to Projector, and is drawn to scale: 1/8" to a Foot.

This side represents the inside of the Projector, from Nodal Point of Objective to Focal Plane (Plate Location), drawn FULL SIZE.

PERSONAL NOTES

THE DIRECT BEAM PROJECTOR

The Direct Beam Projection Principle – projection without lenses – can be traced back to about 121 B.C. and the Chinese "Shadow Theatre."

The German designer, Adolf Linnebach, made the principle popular again about 1910 by painting his setting on a large sheet of glass set in a flared metal box with a lamp at its rear. "Linnebach Lanterns" are still being used, but the many shortcomings have for the most part been overcome in the new Direct Beam Projector in which the settings may be executed in several planes for a better depth illusion.

The Direct Beam Principle, shown in this diagram, is that the closer to the lamp a setting element is interposed, the more diffused and distant it will look on the screen; and the farther from the lamp, the sharper and nearer it will look on the screen.

In the wall of the Lamphouse at left are shown several strips of colored glass. These produce a general diffused color toning of sky and water. Next comes the intermediate, or Middle Distance frame, a sheet of glass upon which the distant coast-line, the clouds and the shadings in the water are painted. Beyond this is the larger Foreground frame which in this case needs no glass. The promontory at left is painted on a cut-out of clear plastic, and the tree on the right is cut-out of black cardboard for a strong silhouette effect.

The principle is thus simple, but its very simplicity is deceptive. A workable unit for lamps up to 1000 watts may be built in any sheet-metal shop but professional results should not be expected from it. For the average sized-stage, with a backdrop projection surface up to 30 x 24 feet, only one lamp type is at this writing practical: the 2100 Watt, 60 Volt General Electric Co. Projection Lamp (Code designations 2100 T 24/8.) which possesses the two essential features: sufficient initial intensity and a small and almost solid filament area (about 1/2" square). But this Lamp also requires a carefully designed, blower-cooled lamphouse with a built-in heat filter, as well as a slowly moving double Color Modifier mechanism within inches of the lamp.

PERSONAL NOTES

The location of the Color Modifier is indicated in the diagram on page 13 by the strips of colored glass in the lamphouse wall. Actually, the strips of progressively graded colors are mounted in two motor-driven frames which can be moved in opposite directions at very slow speeds. This permits gradual transition from day, through sunset, to night, or vice versa, with any suitable setting, an effect mere dimming can not produce. For drifting clouds and other mobile effects, a metal cylinder is mounted to rotate around the lamphouse at varying speeds and in either direction. The cylinder is designed to hold a band of clear plastic upon which clouds and other mobile effects may be painted, or taped on.

The Direct Beam projector is versatile. It may be used without settings as a very efficient cyclorama lighting unit because the Color Modifier will provide not only an always ready softly graded sky, from dark ultramarine at the top to pale turquoise at the horizon, but also the above mentioned transitions between day and night which may be timed so slow as to be practically imperceptible.

Control of speed and direction of Color Modifier and Skydrum is effected through small low-voltage potentiometers at the lighting console.

Other special uses are described under DIRECT BEAM SETTINGS on page 27.

The intensity from a lensless projector decreases by the square of the projection distance. For this reason the Direct Beam projector can not be recommended for long-distance projection until more efficient sources of light become available. A well-designed Direct Beam projector can be adjusted to a spread of 90 degrees but is most efficient within a spread of from 58 to 70 degrees and projection distances up to 30 feet.

The principal advantages of the Direct Beam projector over earlier types of lensless projectors may be summed up as follows:

1. Greater distance between lamp and foreground frame resulting in better definition and clarity of foreground and detail of design.

2. Progressive diffusion as setting elements are interposed closer and closer to the lamp where they are to appear farther and farther away on the screen, thus creating a more convincing illusion of depth.

3. The always-ready color transitions from the slowly and evenly moving Color Modifier near the lamp, and the possibility of executing simple atmospheric backgrounds within a few minutes, and without using glass or paint, by mounting a cut-out skyline of plastic or cardboard in the Intermediate Frame and using the Color Modifier for sky-toning.

4. The possibility of adding drifting clouds and other mobile effects to a setting from the same projector by means of the rotating Skydrum.

5. The advantage of a separate, self-contained lamphouse with forced draft cooling, heat absorbing filter, and color modifier movement, designed as one unit with all vital parts enclosed and protected.

PERSONAL NOTES

SIDE VIEW

FRONT VIEW

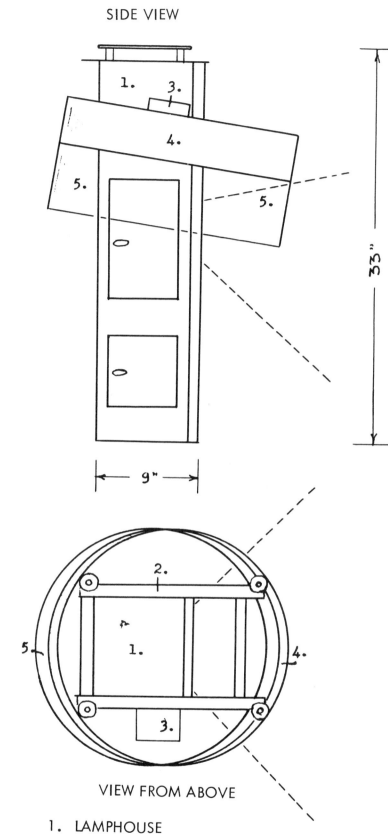

33"

9"

8"

20" DIA

DIRECT BEAM SCENIC PROJECTOR

MAXIMUM SPREAD: 90 DEGREES

DOUBLE COLOR MODIFIER. ALSO
20" DRUM FOR DRIFTING CLOUDS
AND OTHER MOBILE EFFECTS, THE
SPEED & DIRECTION CONTROLLED
FROM ANY REMOTE POINT.

LAMP: 2100 WATTS,   60 VOLTS.
MOTORS & COOLING: 115 VOLTS.
CONTROL CIRCUITS: 6 VOLTS.
COOLING: 50 CFM BLOWER AND
HEAT-ABSORBING GLASS FILTER.

Designed by
THOMAS WILFRED

VIEW FROM ABOVE

1. LAMPHOUSE
2. SKYDRUM CHASSIS
3. SKYDRUM DRIVE MECHANISM
4. 20" METAL SKYDRUM
5. 20" CLEAR PLASTIC DRUM
6. COLOR MODIFIER

PERSONAL NOTES

LOCATION OF PROJECTION EQUIPMENT

In REAR PROJECTION the equipment is generally located on stage floor and in most cases mounted on mobile stands raising the unit to a convenient height for the operator and permitting easy removal when floor space is needed for other purposes. The best location is on a shelf on the back wall mounted at a height which brings the objective up level with the center of the screen (See Comparison Plans) thus eliminating distortion. A projecting booth may here be built around projectors.

In FRONT PROJECTION the equipment must be located high enough over the stage floor for the light beams to clear the acting area (See Comparison Plans). The best location is directly over first light border, just inside fire curtain. There are two installation methods.

SUSPENSION MOUNTING. Recommended where projected settings are used only occasionally. The projectors are clamped onto a 2" pipe batten just long enough to hold the units in their proper locations. This pipe batten is hung directly over the permanent first light border batten but on a separate set of lines with pulleys rigged as close to the light border pulleys as possible. (See lower drawing on Comparison Plans) If the center line on the light border interferes with a projector, a saddle may be rigged on it with a line coming down on either side of the unit in question. For projector-servicing and plate-changing the light border is first lowered to the floor, then the projectors are lowered to a convenient working height on top of the border. If lens projectors are used they must be of the lateral type (See Multiplate Plan) and located at or near center. One or two Direct Beam projectors may be mounted on the same batten, but should be located far enough from the lens unit for their foreground frames to clear the lens beam.

Only the Direct Beam lamphouse with modifier and skydrum is mounted on the projector batten. Middle-distance and Foreground frames are rigged on the next upstage set of lines, in a double frameholder which may be lowered quickly for setting changes. The frame may be removed during the run of plays not using Direct Beam settings and the line set used for scenery. The projectors remain in place since they take up no extra useful space over the light border. Not a single line is sacrificed.

BRIDGE MOUNTING. Recommended where projected settings are used frequently. This installation method is by far the best because the projectors are rigidly mounted on the bridge and instantly available. A good projection bridge also provides storage space and facilities for work on settings, leaving the stage floor entirely free. Additional projectors are easily added. In elaborate productions one or more operators may be stationed at the projectors for rapid changes. Last, but not least, the access hatch may be locked to keep the Idle Curious out. Experience has shown that a surprising percentage of breakage and failure (not to mention outright disappearance of small but vital items) can be traced to the unauthorized person who finds himself alone on the stage and can not resist the temptation to "investigate."

PERSONAL NOTES

THE FRONT PROJECTION BRIDGE

On very large stages, with full flyspace and standard rigging, a steel bridge for scenic projectors and special actor-lighting units (follow spots, etc.) may be hung on two sets of counterweighted cable lines with motor winch for raising and lowering. This arrangement permits removal of entire bridge whenever all of the downstage rigging is needed for elaborate conventional productions.

The smaller the stage, however, the more important the projection equipment will become, and a permanent bridge is recommended, especially where full flyspace is not available. The bridge should extend across the entire stage and be about seven feet deep to permit an operator to move freely without interfering with the projection. The bridge may be an all-metal structure with iron grid flooring, but where fire regulations permit, an excellent bridge may be constructed of wood, with flooring laminated from two thicknesses of 5/8" plywood. Access can be by iron ladder in right or left stage wall, or by door from an upper floor. Both types of entrances should be equipped with locks and kept locked.

It is recommended that one technician be trained to operate the projection equipment. He should have the only key to the bridge and be personally responsible for cleaning, maintenance, and repair.

The plans on the two following pages show an ideal permanent bridge installation on a stage without flyspace, 32' deep, 38' wide, and 29' high. The bridge itself is 7' deep, extends from wall to wall, and is firmly anchored in the masonry on both sides of the proscenium. It has an open slot for the fire curtain and is, in addition, supported by iron hangers from the ceiling. A removable railing runs along upstage edge.

The basic projection equipment consists of one 5000 watt lateral type Muliplate projector located at center and directly inside fire curtain slot, and two 2100 watt Direct Beam projectors located on either side of the lens projector and 15' apart to keep their foreground frames clear of the lens beam. Note that the frames are set parallel to the screen surface to eliminate distortion.

At right and left ends of the bridge are racks for Direct Beam frames, and filing cabinets for 5 x 6" lens projector plates. The Multiplate unit holds ten plates at a time. Twelve different settings may thus be pre-set and used without an operator on the bridge. Worktables with drawers and chest for materials and tools are located by filing racks.

A worklight circuit has lamps on bridge wherever needed, and extra outlets along bridge floor for extension cords and electric tools. This circuit is on 4-way switches, one on bridge, one near ladder on stage.

A house telephone connects the bridge with the control board and the front of the house (for rehearsals).

SMALL STAGE WITH PERMANENT BRIDGE FOR FRONT PROJECTION OF SCENERY

PLAN

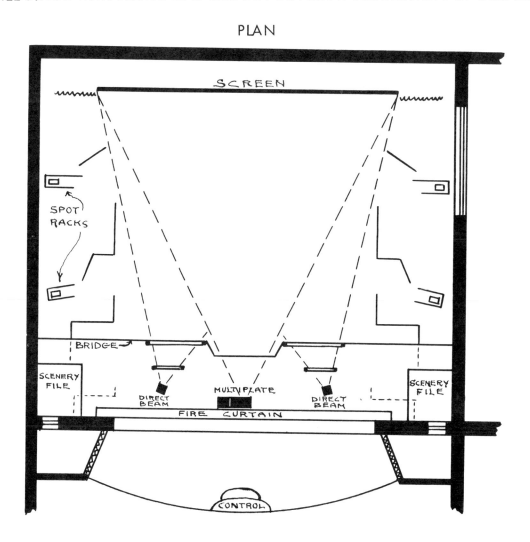

The bridge is seven feet deep and as wide as the stage. The basic equipment consists of one Multiplate projector and two Direct Beam projectors. There is ample room for additional units. Scenery Files and workspace for designing and executing settings are located right & left. The screen is a permanent white plaster surface. A black traveler curtain directly in front of it can cover all or part of it.

A formal set of hinged black wings for side masking is shown on stage. The 4 Spot Racks right and left are suspended from pipes to leave floor space free. Wings and racks are adjustable and will suffice for many stylized productions.

SMALL STAGE WITH PERMANENT BRIDGE FOR FRONT PROJECTION OF SCENERY. LONGITUDINAL SECTION

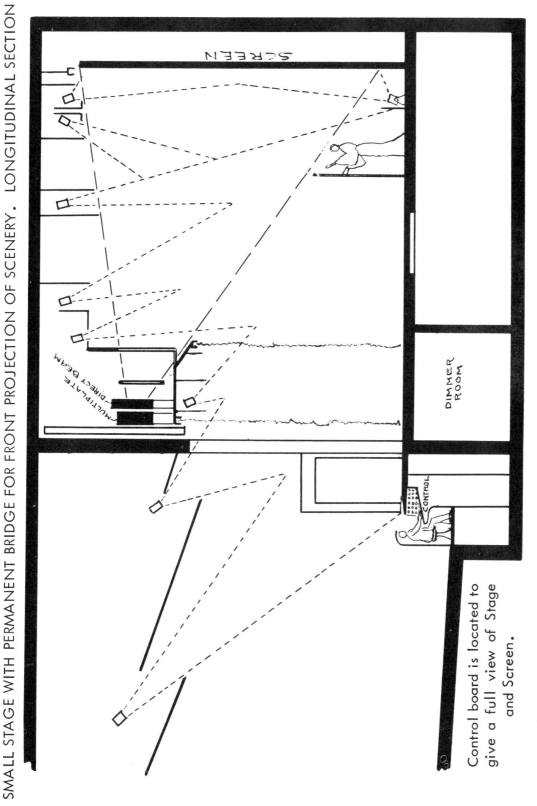

Control board is located to give a full view of Stage and Screen.

Note that actor may move to within his own height of screen without entering projection beam. Note also that all light borders are masked with black on both sides to prevent spills and reflections from reaching the screen surface. The 2 downstage traveler curtains are 6 feet apart. Scenes may thus be played in front of the second traveler while stage is being re-set.

PERSONAL NOTES

The basic projection equipment here consists of only three projectors but there is ample room for extra units as they are needed, such as Focal Stage and Reflection projectors for mobile and fantastic effects on the screen as well as over the acting area (flicker of firelight, sunlight through moving foliage, etc.). It is also advisable to have at least one 1000 watt lens projector with a long-focus objective for intense accents over small areas (windows, street lamps, electric signs on buildings, etc.). A standard stereopticon may serve this purpose.

While a setting is being projected, there will generally be enough reflected light on the bridge for rapid setting changes in other units. For changes during brief blackouts, small shaded blue lamps should be located over projectors and racks. These lamps should be on a circuit separate from the worklights. Another solution is to have the operator wear a kind of miner's cap with a shaded blue flashlight bulb. For such operations a "ready" signal light from bridge to stage manager's desk will be useful.

A black traveler curtain should be located as close to the screen as possible to cover all or part of the white surface during scenes played without setting or with projection on the black surface which can be very effective.

Lightborders and suspended spotracks should be masked with black on both sides to keep spills and reflections from diluting the projection. For the same reason the stage floor should be treated with black paint or stain. Walls and ceiling should be painted flat black. These precautions also help to simplify difficult lighting problems - even where projection is not used - because contrasts can be made sharper, and the space illusion greater.

It has always been important to have the control board located where the operator can see the entire stage as the spectator sees it. With projected settings it becomes even more important. A good location is under center downstage as shown on the plans on the preceding pages. In the University Playhouse in Seattle, Washington, the author located the board in a room back of the last orchestra row. Time has proved this an excellent location because the man at the board should now be an artist, able to blend setting and actor-lighting together to form an integrated Visual Accompaniment to speech and action. As the art of light has been named Lumia, we may fittingly call the light-player "Lumianist." The author favors a simple manual control board requiring some skill of the lumianist, and granting him in return the same latitude for personal interpretation we now grant the musician. Only in this way can the visual accompaniment become a living thing.

UNUSUAL PROBLEMS

The following pages show projection installations on stages presenting different problems in size and proportion. In most cases a solution can be found, and not necessarily an expensive one.

PERSONAL NOTES

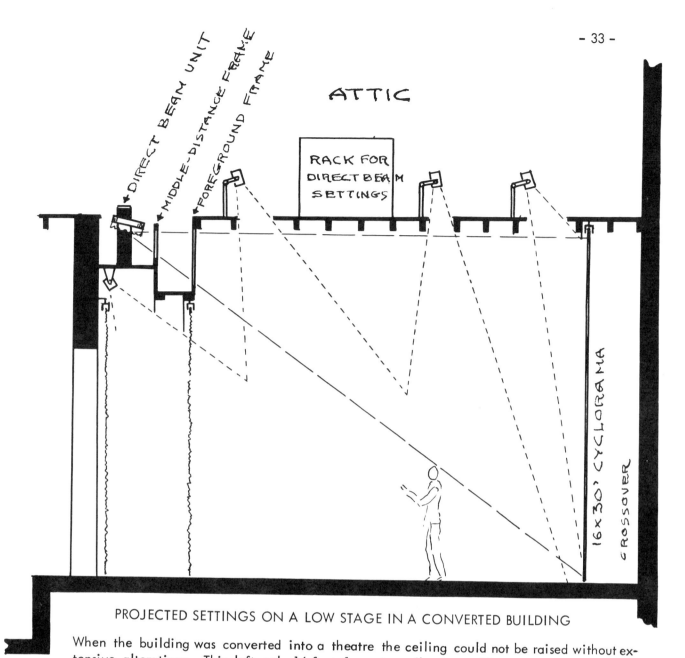

ATTIC

DIRECT BEAM UNIT

MIDDLE-DISTANCE FRAME

FOREGROUND FRAME

RACK FOR DIRECT BEAM SETTINGS

16 x 30' CYCLORAMA

CROSSOVER

PROJECTED SETTINGS ON A LOW STAGE IN A CONVERTED BUILDING

When the building was converted into a theatre the ceiling could not be raised without extensive alterations. This left only 16 feet from stage floor to ceiling joists, but above the ceiling was an unused attic. The special problem was solved by using the attic as a projection bridge. An open well was cut in the ceiling just inside proscenium to hold a 2100 Watt Direct Beam projector and its frames. The upper projection beam just missed the ceiling joists, and the light borders had to be located in the attic over long slots in the ceiling, the slots thus also serving as masking. One operator in the attic, with the storage rack at his elbow, can now change the settings in a matter of seconds. The arrangement also permits easy servicing of both the projector and the light borders. The cyclorama is only 16' high but spans the entire 30' of stage width and thus permits the projection of impressive settings of "Cinemascope" proportions. A lateral scene dock holds two wagon stages, and scenes may be played against the second traveler curtain while settings are changed.

PERSONAL NOTES

FRONT PROJECTION ON A SPACE-STAGE WITH A FULL CURVED 90 X 50 FEET CYCLORAMA

EQUIPMENT: TWO DIRECT BEAM PROJECTORS, LOCATED ELEVEN FEET APART AND ADJUSTED TO A 90-DEGREE HORIZONTAL SPREAD

ONE CENTRALLY LOCATED TEN-PLATE LATERAL TYPE MULTIPLATE PROJECTOR

PROJECTION DISTANCE: 29 FEET.   TOTAL CYCLORAMA AREA: 4,500 SQUARE FEET.

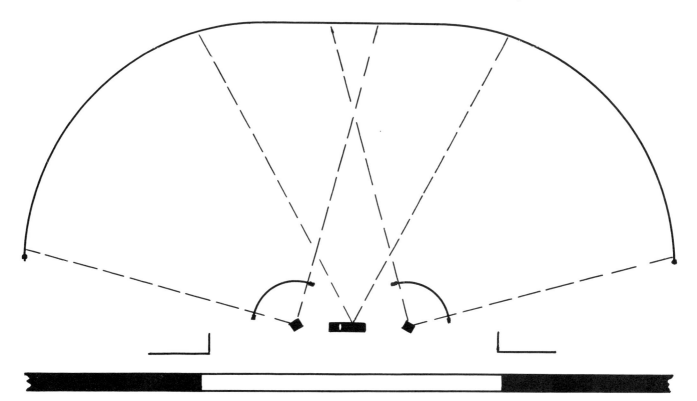

The two Direct Beam Projectors are swivel-mounted, and are here seen swung out to cover the entire ninety feet of cyclorama spread, with a five-foot overlap in center. The two images may therefore be joined so gradually that no juncture is discernible. The two foreground frames are curved to match cyclorama, thus eliminating distortion.

The Multiplate projector may be used in conjunction with the two Direct Beam units for accents and detail in the central area.

When a production requires only backdrop-size projections, the two Direct Beam units are swung in so that both cover the same 30 foot central area already covered by the Multiplate unit. Black traveler curtains on curved tracks are then pulled in to cover the unused side areas of the cyclorama.   This arrangement permits the use of twelve different settings by remote control – one merging into the next, if desired.

THE HEPTARENA THEATRE

It has hitherto been impossible to use pictorial backgrounds in the Arena Theatre. Now, by means of projection, truly impressive settings, static or mobile, realistic or fantastic, may be thrown around audience and actors alike.

The Heptarena, designed by the author, is the first of this type. (See opposite page.) The walls of the heptagonal hall are covered by seven 24 x 16' white screens 1, separated by dark columns 2. From each column a concealed scenic projector 3 can cover the screen diametrically opposite with easy and distortion-free angles. From the dark ceiling any number of "invisible-source" spots and floods 4 can light the central arena 5 from any practical angle. The arena is 26' in diameter and equipped with two trap-elevators 6, each large enough to bring up a pre-set unit of props during action on the other half of arena. The seating area is divided into seven sections A - G of 50 seats each. All aisles 8 lead to exits 9. Back of the upper tier of seats a six-foot parapet 10 conceals a continuous passage 11 for the actors, from which they can follow the progress of the play and time their entrances along the seven aisles (or appear over the parapet at any point). In addition, a small platform 12 over each exit permits balcony appearances. The control board is located behind the parapet at 13. Sections B - G are identical, but section A has a stage 14 behind it, and an orchestra pit 15 below it. By removing seats and parapet section, and by raising the projection screen, an 18' deep stage with a 10' forestage is ready to be used as an extension of the arena, or by itself, with or without orchestra pit. In this last case the arena may be used for seating (89 seats). Change-overs from any set-up to another may be effected in one hour or less. The seven scenic projectors 3 are located in a closed circular gallery 16 with a scenery file by each projector, and workspace for plate designing and processing. Spaces 17 under arena and stage contain dressing, prop, and costume rooms. This plan shows a small Heptarena of 350 seats, suitable for Educational Theatre work. (The idea is fully as suitable for a house seating 3,500.) The extreme flexibility of design will permit the following rapid conversions.

ARENA ONLY. All 7 sections identical. Projected settings on all 7 screens. (350 seats)

ARENA & STAGE. Classical & Spectacle. Section A becomes forestage and steps, joining arena and stage 14 into one large acting area with several levels. Projected settings on 6 screens and back wall of stage. Orchestra pit 15 may be partially or fully open (for chorus) or covered. (300 seats)

STAGE ONLY. Plays. Stage 14 and forestage in section A as acting area. Seats in sections B & G turned to face stage. Seating in arena. Settings on back wall of stage. 6 house screens used for decorative projection. (389 seats)

STAGE & ORCHESTRA PIT. Operas & Musicals. Stage & Forestage as acting area. Pit 15 open, holding full orchestra. Seating in arena. (389 seats)

SMALL PLATFORM. Recitals & Lectures. All 7 sections identical. Trap elevator 6 raised three feet over arena level. Seating in remainder of arena. Decorative projection on all 7 screens. (415 seats)

The Heptarena will appear to the spectators as a large pergola supported by seven dark columns and opening up on space in all directions. Acoustical properties have been carefully worked out. In quick succession it may be turned into a cathedral, a Greek temple, a primeval forest, or, for one of Shakespeare's plays, the old Globe Theatre of London. If no settings are desired, rich brocade curtains in heavy folds may be projected.

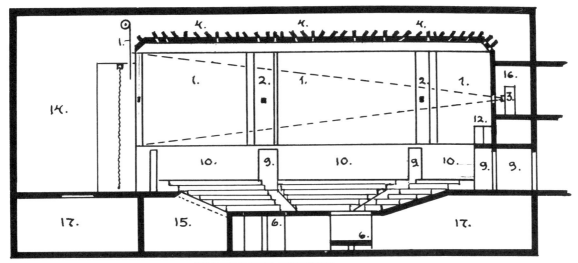

TRANSVERSE SECTION

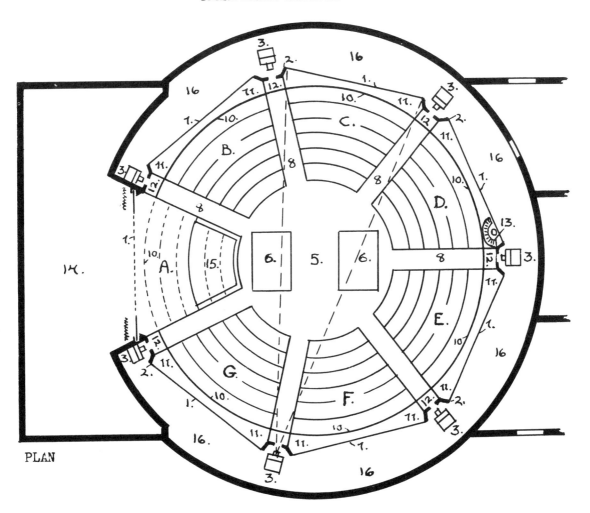

PLAN

THE HEPTARENA THEATRE

An Arena Theatre designed for the use of projected settings surrounding audience and actors alike with a continuous pictorial background. Stage 14 and Section A may be combined with arena to form one large acting area with several levels. A full Orchestra Pit is available with any of the set-ups.

Designed by Thomas Wilfred, Art Institute of Light, West Nyack, New York.

TWO PROJECTED SETTINGS FROM THE UNIVERSITY OF WASHINGTON PLAYHOUSE, SEATTLE

DIRECT BEAM SETTING for "THE DREAM AND THE DEED"
By John A. Conway and Alanson Davis

The trees were painted on clear plastic in the foreground frame, the mountains in the middle-distance frame. A change from day through sunset to night was effected with the color modifier and controlled from the lighting console.

A MULTIPLATE SETTING for "THE MARRIAGE OF FIGARO"
By John A. Conway

The setting was executed in color on 11 x 14 inch illustration board, then photographed on a 5 x 7 inch Ektachrome film with the camera located at the same downward angle that the projector is tilted down toward the white backdrop on the stage. The distorted image on the film then produced a corrected setting.

PERSONAL NOTES

DESIGNING AND EXECUTING SETTINGS FOR LENS PROJECTORS

Whenever possible, a lens projector should be located center stage to avoid compound distortion. In Rear Projection the unit may be located to face the exact center of the screen, thus eliminating all distortion.

In Front Projection, from batten or bridge, the projector generally tips down about 15 degrees. The top of the screen is thus much closer to the projector than the bottom, and a rectangular plate image would produce a keystone-shaped image on the screen, widest at the bottom. To correct this distortion the image on the plate must be keystone-shaped to compensate. How much? The simplest method for determining the correct distortion is as follows. With the projector in its proper location, place a clear glass slide in the plateholder and bring the lamp up to one-quarter intensity. Now insert a china-marking pencil to the glass slide and mark off the four corners while looking at the screen. Pull out the plate and mount black masking tape along the four sides to meet the corner marks. Insert again and keep moving tape strips until you have a perfect rectangle of light over the desired screen area. The framed keystone-shaped area on the plate is now your effective picture area. Cut several sheets of thin clear plastic, lay them over the plate and trace the picture area on the plastic with India ink. In the following we shall assume that you use the 5 x 6" plate size, the most practical, and that you have executed a drawing of the setting to be processed in the plate proportions, for example 20 x 24". The transfer from drawing to plate may be done by several methods.

1. Photographing the drawing in color on an Ektachrome or similar film, and mounting this film between two cover-glasses.
2. Photographing the drawing on a black and white negative, printing a positive plate or film by contact, and coloring this by hand.
3. Reducing the drawing to plate size on tissue paper, placing this paper under a clear glass slide in retouching stand, and painting the entire setting by hand. Instead of glass, the setting may be painted on a sheet of thin clear plastic and mounted between glasses.
4. For simple outlines, or non-objective and decorative effects, lay the tissue reduction under a clear plate in retouching stand, make overlapping cut-outs of colored gelatine and seal with a second clear glass plate.

The above procedures may be varied and combined, but in all of them one general rule must be followed. The final plate must not be dense, it must transmit as much light as consistent with good quality, or your setting will not be able to hold its own against unavoidable reflections from the acting area. Study a set of professional lantern slides and note how almost transparent they are. You can always use the dimmer on a too bright setting but you can not add extra intensity if your plate arrests too much of the initial light. Have this in mind when you make your drawings, and instruct the photographer about it. Only when you want intense coloring in a night scene can you afford density, and you must then balance the actor lighting to match it. Another factor is that a dense plate converts the arrested light into heat which may crack the plate.

Make at least one extra copy of every setting. Consider the first one a practice plate and also a handy spare in case of damage. Have dust-proof filing cabinets for all plates, in the studio as well as at the projectors.

PERSONAL NOTES

1. THE EKTACHROME PROCESS. Execute the setting in full color on a 20 x 24" illustration board and to exact screen proportions. Use a 5 x 7" view camera and tape one of the plastic distortion charts over the ground glass upside-down. Mount drawing right side-up on a tiltable easel and keep adjusting easel and camera until drawing outlines register exactly with distortion outlines on ground glass. Illuminate the drawing with the proper lamps for the color film to be used and exclude all daylight from room. Stop down to smallest lens aperture and expose one or two points over meter reading for greater translucency. Make at least two exposures of every setting. Cut 1/2" off each end of the color film and seal between two cover glasses.

2. HAND-COLORED PHOTOGRAPHIC POSITIVE. Proceed as above, but execute the drawing in black and white, approximating color-values in grey. Use a suitable black and white photographic film or plate in camera, giving it a slight overexposure. Make black and white positive film or plate by contact printing from negative and develop. Use no acid in fixing bath. Make a second positive when the result on the first has been analyzed. Set the dry positive in a retouching stand and color with lantern slide colors (Kodak Book Colors are excellent). Before painting treat the dry emulsion on positive with diluted oxalic acid (or undiluted saliva) to make the colors "take." Use very diluted colors to begin with.

Slide-coloring is not difficult but requires considerable practice and patience on the part of the beginner. A well-lighted photographer's retouching stand is indispensable. Make a dozen or more positives of your first setting and keep practicing and testing the results in projector.

If your plate projector is equipped with color modifier, you may in some cases leave the sky area blank and use the modifier for sky hues.

3. HAND-PAINTED SLIDES. Reduce drawing to plate size and distort to register with plastic distortion chart on tissue paper or architect's tracing paper and place this drawing under a 5 x 6" clear glass plate in the retouching stand. The painting is here done on the untreated glass surface and the colors used must have a lacquer or similar base to adhere. Ordinary lamp-dip colors are generally satisfactory and may be purchased from any stagelighting concern in pint bottles. One or two pints of thinner should be ordered with the colors because here, again, density is to be avoided. Considerable practice is again recommended because the colors are quick-drying and can not be worked over, but any unsatisfactory area may be scraped clean and painted again. It is important that the final result is even and transparent; frosted or blurred areas create fog and diffusion on screen. Mica plates may be substituted for glass. Colors may be applied by air-brush but this involves expensive equipment.

4. GELATINE CUT-OUTS BETWEEN COVERGLASSES. Proceed as for hand-painting but use colored gelatines, single or in graded overlapping layers. Good, slightly humidified gelatine should be used. Straight and curved scissors are the best tools. Fasten cut-outs with clear cement to plate edges. Sky and water areas on hand-pained plates may be executed by this method. Remove all dust and fingerprints before sealing on the cover plate.

If time or facilities are lacking for plate-making, have a local photographer make the black and white positives. Then send these, with an adequate color sketch, to a studio specializing in lantern slide coloring.

PERSONAL NOTES

DESIGNING AND EXECUTING SETTINGS FOR THE DIRECT BEAM PROJECTOR

The great advantage here is that a setting may be executed by degrees, and changes and improvements made at any stage in the process. If you are fortunate enough to have the unit installed on a permanent bridge, with work table and tools at your elbow, you may actually create the setting on the screen as you go along by having the projector on at low intensity.

First comes the basic color-toning of large areas, such as sky and water. This may be accomplished with the Color Modifier at the lamphouse which normally is operated from the board but may also be moved by hand at the projector until the desired basic toning has been achieved. A sheet of glass or plastic in the Middle-distance Frame is used for distant cloud banks and other sky modifications unless drifting clouds are in order. In this case the Skydrum is tipped down into the beam and a prepared strip of cloud images is taped onto the plastic lower part of the drum.

Distant horizon lines and far-away objects are painted or taped onto the Middle-distance frame which is located about 18" out from the lamphouse. If only a simple horizon line is needed, such as a mountain range in blue haze, a full sheet of plastic is not necessary. The contour is cut as a long strip of blue Cinabex, or painted clear plastic, and taped into the otherwise empty frame.

The larger Foreground Frame is located 3 - 4 feet from lamphouse and reserved for setting elements which are to appear nearer and sharper. This frame needs a full sheet of plastic only for interiors, street scenes, and settings with little or no sky area. In most cases there will be only a tree, part of a building, or a groundrow and these may be cut out of fairly heavy clear plastic, painted, and taped into the frame. If these design elements need support use very thin steel or brass wire laced taut across frame. For elements in silhouette use black cardboard.

Increase the intensity from time to time in order to evaluate the progress. When the setting is completed go through all changes and transitions used in the scene. This may reveal further modifications to be made. Study the setting from various seats in the house with at least some of the actor lighting on.

For the one-plane Linnebach Lantern, the entire setting must be painted on the large sheet of glass in the front opening of the housing. A softly graded sky is difficult to paint here. It may, however, be achieved by taping layers of colored gelatine or Cinabex onto the glass.

The 2100 watt lamp used in most Direct Beam projectors has a rated life of only 50 hours because of its intense concentrated filament arrangement, but its life may be more than doubled if it is burned a little under full intensity during normal conditions. This rule applies to all lamps.

PERSONAL NOTES

SPECIAL EFFECT ATTACHMENTS FOR THE DIRECT BEAM PROJECTOR

MULTIBEAM LENS. A patented attachment consisting of juxtaposed cylindrical lenses is supplied with the Direct Beam projectors built at the Art Institute of Light. The attachment fits over the Modifier aperture and sends out from five to seven horizontal or vertical beams spaced one inch apart at the lens. Each beam then spreads to cover the entire screen. As a result every unit of setting or color is seen on the screen in several juxtaposed and overlapping repetitions. By merely spacing vertical strips of black cardboard in the Foreground Frame, a row of solid-looking fluted columns can be projected. Impressive static or mobile fantastic backgrounds may also be executed.

ROTATING PLATFORM. For mobile effects, especially in connection with the Multibeam lens, a variable-speed rotating platform, 12-16" in diameter, may be located below the beam of light between Modifier and Middle-distance Frame. A three-dimensional and fairly open construction of curved or other shapes may then be rotated slowly to create an effect of waxing and waning multiple forms. In connection with this the skydrum may be lowered all the way into the beam and a plastic strip with a color sequence painted on it moved horizontally right or left.

ROTATING DISCS. For mobile effects, such as fire, mist, underwater vistas, and also purely fantastic and non-objective backgrounds, one or more discs of glass, Mica, or plastic may be rotated in the beam of light close to the Color Modifier. The number, location and velocities of such discs will vary with the effect desired. Here experimentation is in order.

MOVING SETTING. In certain plays it is indicated that the action move in one direction or another during the playing of a scene, and that the setting must show the change of location, as for example in PARSIFAL, when Gurnemanz leads Parsifal from the forest to the temple. This effect is generally achieved with a long painted slide which is drawn slowly through the focal plane of a lens projector, but it may also be projected by means of a Direct Beam unit with a large wheel rotating horizontally under the lamphouse. The setting elements are mounted along the rim and adjusted to move through the beam close to the Foreground Frame. This procedure was used by Professor Conway at the University Playhouse in Seattle, the first theatre in the United States to have a stage especially designed for front projection. The play was DR. KNOCK by Louis Jouvet. In act one an automobile is to carry four people through the mountains while they comment on the scenery. The car breaks down and is then pushed along by the chauffeur. The car on the stage was constructed to have the wheels turn as the setting moved. When the car stopped, so did the setting. (See Players Magazine, Jan. '54, p. 90)

It is also possible to create an illusion of motion toward or away from a location. This is achieved by mounting the lamphouse on an overhead track. As the lamphouse is moved toward the stationary setting frames the entire setting expands and gives the spectator the feeling of moving tight in through the proscenium. The opposite effect is created by moving the lamphouse away from the frames.

PERSONAL NOTES

THE FINAL TEST -- THE ACTUAL PRODUCTION

Let us say you have just had scenic projection equipment installed on your stage. You have designed and executed settings for the first play. One late night you have tried them on the screen and they looked fine.

Now comes the first stage rehearsal. Spots, floods, and borders are turned on to light the actors. Your heart sinks. Spills from the lighting units and reflections from floor, flats and props all but wash out your handiwork. With painted and lighted scenery these spills were never noticed. Now you will have to do something about it.

You must inspect, adjust, and sometimes remodel every single unit for actor lighting until it lights the desired area and nothing else!

Let us say you have a border with a little of everything, large and small spots with plain or Fresnel lenses, clusters of G 40s with color frames, all of them spilling white light right and left, brightly illuminating the unpainted back of the next downstage border or drop and sending a diffused glow all over the screen, especially over the bottom where you want it least of all. If the lighting units themselves can not be made light-tight in unwanted directions with shields and louvers, you must do what has already been indicated on the longitudinal section of a stage on page 19. You must hang black teasers on both sides of each border and adjust them in height until all spills and reflections have been eliminated. To test the result, turn on all actor lighting used in the production, get down on your hands and knees and crawl across the stage close to the screen, all the time looking upward. On this journey you should not be able to see a single source of light, be it from above, from sides, or from auditorium beams. Nor should you be able to see any lighted surface facing upstage, be it backs of tormentors, flats, or setpieces. Footlights should, of course, never be used with projected settings.

Next comes the stage floor, often left unpainted and shiny. It presents a large surface and reflects a tremendous amount of light up to the screen. Have it sanded and give it a liberal treatment with black stain or paint. When possible cover the stage with a dark groundcloth and cover that most critical area: the last four feet near the screen with dark cocomatting. It will also be helpful to paint the side walls flat black. These precautions should eliminate all of the unwanted light.

Now try again. You will find that your settings can easily hold their own against normal actor lighting. If not, look for the following causes.

1. Insufficient initial intensity in projector.
2. Setting plate too dense, absorbing too much light.
3. Actor lighting too strong for the mood of the scene being played. (In an outdoor night scene the actors should be lit to give the illusion that they are outdoors at night, etc.)

It is all a matter of judicious balance. A scenic designer is essentially an accompanist who only on rare occasions can justify a solo passage.

If at the final curtain no one in the audience has realized that the settings were projected, well - so much the better!

PERSONAL NOTES

GLOSSARY

ANASTIGMATIC OBJECTIVE. A compound optical assembly consisting of several elements mounted in a metal barrel. By using different glass sorts (crown and flint) and different curvatures (convex and concave) the optical imperfections inherent in each glass sort and curvature are balanced to neutralize each other and thus transmit to the screen a sharp and undistorted enlargement of the plate image in the focal plane.

ANGLE OF COVERAGE. The relation between the focal length of an objective and the diameter of the circular field it is capable of transmitting.

APERTURE. The effective diameter of an objective. Measured by the ratio of its focal length to its diameter.

CONDENSER. One of several lenses used in a lens projector to pick up the light from the lamp and to refract it into a beam of sufficient diameter to cover the entire plate in the focal plane and then to converge the beam to a nodal point coinciding with the nodal point of the objective.

DISTORTION. On most stages it is necessary to project at an angle to the screen plane, generally downward, in order to clear the acting area. A rectangular plate in the projector would therefore produce a distorted screen image, increasing in size with the distance from projector to screen. In order to achieve a rectangular screen image, the plate image must be distorted to compensate for the varying projection distances from top to bottom of screen. SIMPLE DISTORTION occurs when the projector is located over the center of the stage. COMPOUND DISTORTION when the projector is also off-center, right or left. Extreme angles should be avoided.

OPTICAL ELEMENT. Any single lens forming part of an optical system.

FIRST-SURFACE MIRROR. A mirror having its reflecting surface facing the beam it reflects. A polished metal mirror is thus first-surface, a glass mirror only when its coating is applied to the outward surface and highly polished. An ordinary glass mirror has its reflecting surface under the glass and this produces double reflection – one from the coated undersurface and a weaker one from the upper glass surface. For this reason a mirror forming part of an optical surface must be first-surface.

FOCAL LENGTH of an objective. The distance between its nodal point and its focal plane when a sharp image is transmitted. The shorter the focal length, the wider the angle of projection and the larger the screen image.

FOCAL PLANE in a lens projector. The plane in which the plate containing the setting image (the slide) is inserted in the projector. It should be near the last condenser element but not too close, or surface imperfections on the condenser will appear with the screen image.

NODAL POINT in an optical system. The point where all transmitted light rays converge and cross, thus reversing the transmitted image.

OPTICAL AXIS. The centerline through an optical system.

PERSONAL NOTES

BIBLIOGRAPHY

Books:

Alton, John. PAINTING WITH LIGHT. New York: Macmillan, 1949.

Bentham, Frederick. THE ART OF STAGE LIGHTING. London: Pitman, 1968.

Bellman, Willard F. LIGHTING THE STAGE: ART AND PRACTICE. San Francisco: Chandler, 1967.

Bongar, Emmet W. THE THEATRE STUDENT: PRACTICAL STAGE LIGHTING. New York: Richard Rosen Press, 1971.

Burris-Meyer, Harold and Edward C. Cole. SCENERY FOR THE THEATRE. Boston: Little, Brown, 1971.

Burris-Meyer, Harold and Edward C. Cole. THEATRES AND AUDITORIUMS, 2nd edition. New York: Van Nostrand, 1964.

Cheney, Sheldon. STAGE DECORATION. New York: Benjamin Blom, 1967.

Fuchs, Theodore. STAGE LIGHTING. New York: Benjamin Blom, 1963.

Goffin, Peter. STAGE LIGHTING FOR AMATEURS. Chicago: Coach House Press, 1955.

Heffner, Hubert, Samuel Selden and Hunton D. Sellman. MODERN THEATRE PRACTICE, 4th, edition. New York: Appleton-Century-Crofts, 1959.

Kook, Edward. IMAGES IN LIGHT FOR THE LIVING THEATRE. New York: Drama Book Shop, 1963.

Lounsbury, Warren C. THEATRE BACKSTAGE FROM A to Z. Seattle: University of Washington, 1967.

McCandless, Stanley. A METHOD OF LIGHTING THE STAGE. New York: Theatre Arts Books, 1958.

McCandless, Stanley. A SYLLABUS OF STAGE LIGHTING. New York: Drama Book Specialists, 1964.

Parker, W. Oren and Harvey K. Smith. SCENE DESIGN AND STAGE LIGHTING. New York: Holt, Rinehart and Winston, 1963.

Philippi, Herbert. STAGECRAFT AND SCENE DESIGN. Boston: Houghton, Mifflin, 1953.

Pilbrow, Richard. STAGE LIGHTING. New York: Rinehold, 1970.

Rubin, Joel E. and Leland H. Watson. THEATRICAL LIGHTING PRACTICE. New York: Theatre Arts Books, 1968.

Santos, Louisa. PROJECTED SCENERY FOR THE SCHOOL STAGE. Boston: Walter Baker, 1949.

Selden, Samuel and Hunton D. Sellman. STAGE SCENERY AND LIGHTING. Boston: Appleton-Century-Crofts, 1959.

Williams, R. G. THE TECHNIQUE OF STAGE LIGHTING, 2nd edition. London: Pitman, 1960.

Magazine Articles:

PLAYERS MAGAZINE
Conway, John A. PROJECTED SCENERY. March, 1952.
Conway, John A. BUILD YOUR OWN DIRECT BEAM. January, 1953.
Conway, John A. MAKING ORIGINALS FOR PHOTOGRAPHIC SLIDES. May, 1953.
Conway, John A. DRAWING DISTORTION. October, 1953.
Conway, John A. MOVING SCENIC PROJECTION. January, 1954.
Wilfred, Thomas. THE DESIGNER ENTERS THE RING (Heptarena.) November, 1953.

EDUCATIONAL THEATRE MAGAZINE
Wilfred, Thomas. THE PROJECTED SETTING. May, 1954.
Rubin, J. et. al. THE PROJECTED SETTING, A SYMPOSIUM. October, 1954.

WORLD THEATRE (International Theatre Institute Magazine)
Unruh, Walther. PROJECTED SCENERY. Vol. 2, #4. Spring, 1953.
Rubin & Watson. CONCERNING PROJECTED SCENERY. Vol. 3, #4. Autumn, 1954.

THEATRE ARTS MAGAZINE
Pichel, Irving. LIGHTING. September, 1925.
Wilfred, Thomas. PROMETHEUS AND MELPOMENE. September, 1928. (Viking Production)

ENCYCLOPAEDIA BRITANNICA. 14th Edition.
Wilfred, Thomas. STAGE DESIGN (Part) Volume 21, pp. 289 – 290.

Press comments on the production of Ibsen's THE VIKINGS AT HELGELAND at the Goodman Theatre, Chicago. Directed by Thomas Wood Stevens. Projected settings and visual accompaniment by Thomas Wilfred. The production broke the box office record of the house and had the longest run of any play in the Goodman Theatre's life as a repertory theatre.

Ashton Stevens, in The Chicago Herald Examiner:
"The clavilux gave to "The Vikings" such a sea and sky and firelight as Ibsen never dreamed. Wagner, you feit, would have given his life - or that of the mad Ludwig - to have had the clavilux for his "Walkure" alone.

"It was the first full enjoyment of this instrument in a dramatic performance, and, as was said when Wilfred played in conjunction with the Philadelphia Orchestra, Who knows but that history was made."

C. J. Bulliet, in The Chicago Evening Post:
"Not since the electric bulb supplanted the old gas lamp in the theatre has anything so important happened in the theatre as the introduction of Thomas Wilfred and the clavilux in the production of Ibsen's "Vikings" at the Goodman Theatre.

"The effects seem to come out of nothingness - as magically as sunlight and moonlight emerge from the ether. Wilfred accompanies the players as an expert pianist accompanies a singer. His lights are never still, and yet they never obtrude."

The Chicago American:
"Here indeed is a "fourth dimension" in emotion that has never before been achieved in such dramatic form."

The Chicagoan:
"The illusion of these light effects has the enchantment of poetry."

See also comments on this production in the 14th edition of
ENCYCLOPAEDIA BRITANNICA, Vol. 21, pp 289-290.

BIOGRAPHICAL NOTES ON THOMAS WILFRED

1889. Born in Nestvad, Denmark。

1905. First experimented with light and color.

1905 - 1911. Studied art and music in Copenhagen, Paris and London, and became a singer of old songs and player of the 12-string Arch-lute.

1914. Royal Command performance at the English Court, London.

1915. Royal Command performance at the Danish Court, Copenhagen。

1916. Came to the United States and continued career as a singer in order to gather funds for his experiments in the use of light as an independent art medium.

1919. Designed the first important instrument for the performance of silent visual compositions, naming this instrument the Clavilux, and the new art form Lumia.

1922. Played the first public Lumia recitals on the Clavilux in New York City.

1922 - 1925. Played Lumia recitals all over the United States and Canada.

1925. First European tour. Lumia acclaimed in Paris, London and Copenhagen, where the Danish government arranged a special recital in the Royal Theatre。

1926. Appeared as soloist with the Philadelphia Orchestra under Stokowski, playing his own visual setting for "Sheherazade" by Rimsky Korsakoff.

1927. Composed and performed a visual setting for Ibsen's play, "The Vikings", at the Goodman Theatre in Chicago。 The production broke all records.

1925 - 1929. On tour with a new Clavilux over the United States and Canada.

1929. Contributed articles to the 14th edition of Encyclopaedia Brittanica. Executed the first projected mural, 21 x 210 feet, in Holtel Sherman, Chicago。 The mural retains its original beauty after more than 30 years of constant use.

1930. Founded the Art Institute of Light, a non-profit research center for the development of Lumia, the Art of Light。 Directed the Institute's theatre and studios in New York City, 1933 - 1943, also playing and lecturing.

1943. Museum of Modern Art acquired recorded composition, "Vertical Sequence。"

1943 - 1945. War work as editor and announcer in the Danish department of the U.S. Office of War Information.

1946. Decorated by King Christian X of Denmark.

1947 - 1950. On tour with lecture-recital "New Frontier in Art." Worked on first textbook, "Lumia, the Art of Light." Contributed two articles to Journal of Aesthetics - "Light and the Artist" and "Composing in Lumia."

1951. Designed the lighting equipment for the University of Washington Playhouse - the first theatre in the United States especially designed for projected scenery and keyboard control of all lighting.

1957. Designed the lighting equipment for the University of Georgia's new Center Theatre in Athens, Ga. Published technical manual "Projected Scenery."

1958. The Metropolitan Museum of Art in New York City acquired "Counterpoint in Space, Op. 146 for its permanent collection of American art.

1959. Completed "Study in Depth, Op. 152," 6 x 9 feet, now installed as the focal point in the Clairol reception room, 666 Fifth Avenue, New York City.

1960. Completed "Spacetime Study, Op. 153" and "Spacedrift, Op. 154."

1964. Museum of Modern Art installed permanent exhibit, "Lumia Suite, Op. 158," a 12 minute projected composition which its creator described as "an abstract visual drama of form, color and motion" and which The New York Times called "a musical symphony...of shapes and colors that swim soundlessly over a 6 x 8 foot projection screen."